Helping Children See Themselves In History

This Eyeseeme book belongs to:

_____

__

This Story can be found in
The Book of Genesis chapters 37 - 46

This book is dedicated to all the mothers and fathers that are seeking to teach their children to see themselves in the Bible. I pray that it is as beneficial to your children as it has been for mine.

The Story of Joseph

By

Pamela Blair

Illustrated by Stephone Handy

Fifth Ribb Publishing
6951 Olive Blvd
St. Louis, Missouri, 63130

Copyright © 2016 by Eyeseeme, LLC
All Rights Reserved. This book or any portion thereof may not be reproduced or used in any manner whatsoever without the express written permission of the publisher except for the use of brief quotations in a book review.

Printed in the United States of America
First Edition, 2012
Library of Congress Control Number: 2011943263
ISBN: 978-0984810468

Jacob lived in the land of Canaan, the land promised to his grandfather Abraham by God. God promised that the land would belong to Abraham and his descendants. Jacob was now a father of 12 young sons. The young men would become the foundation of the 12 tribes of Israel, the beginning of God's chosen people, the Israelite family.

Jacob's eleventh son, Joseph, was Jacob's favorite. Jacob had known since Joseph's birth that there was something special about him, and he sensed that someday Joseph would serve God well and be obedient. One day Jacob decided to give Joseph a special gift for always listening and being a good son. He made him a coat. Not just any coat, but a coat with as many colors as you can imagine. When the older brothers saw this, they became very jealous, and began excluding Joseph from everything. They hardly took him along when they went places, and they treated him unkindly, often speaking to him harshly. Joseph often felt hurt, but he loved his older brothers and wanted so very much for them to like him.

One night Joseph had a dream, and he immediately told his brothers and his father. Not knowing exactly what it meant, he said calmly, "Last night, I dreamed that we were all gathering and tying up bunches of grain out in the field. Then suddenly, my bunch stood up, while all of yours gathered around and bowed down to mine." His older brothers' faces flushed with anger and dislike, but Joseph continued. "I had another dream in which the sun, moon, and eleven stars bowed down to me."

Now the brothers' jealousy changed to hate, and they shouted at Joseph. "Do you think that you are so special and better than us?" they screamed. "We will never bow down to you!"

One morning not long after, four of Joseph's brothers—Reuben, Judah, Simeon, and Levi—went out in the field to do their usual chores. Like many other families of the time, they lived on a very large plot of land, a plot many, many miles long. The young men were gone for what seemed an exceptionally long time, and Jacob became worried about his sons, wondering what was taking them so long. Jacob asked Joseph to go find the four brothers.

As Joseph got closer to his brothers, they saw his beautiful coat and began to conspire a plan. "Let's kill this dreamer," one whispered.

Reuben, the oldest, said, "We don't have to kill him. Let's just throw him into this pit." Rueben planned to come back and rescue Joseph later, though he kept this to himself.

When Joseph came near, the brothers grabbed him, pulled off his coat, and threw him into a dreadful pit. Joseph screamed, but no one came to help.

Rueben returned to his chores, while the others remained close to the pit. An hour went by and the brothers soon spotted a group of strangers approaching on camels. The strangers were Ishmaelite merchants selling various products from their native land, Egypt. "We can sell our brother Joseph to the strangers, and he would be gone from us forever," said Judah. The other two loved the idea, and so they sold Joseph to the merchants for 20 pieces of silver.

When Rueben returned from working, he looked into the pit. "Where is Joseph?" he asked.

"We sold him to some Ishmaelite merchants," said the others. "He will be okay."

Rueben cried out, and tore his clothing off of his body, "NO! Why? He is our brother."

On the way home, the four brothers grew frightened of what their father might say. They decided to take blood from a dead animal and smear it all over Joseph's coat. Nervously they planned what they would say to their dad very carefully so that he would believe that a wild animal had killed Joseph.

Upon hearing the tale, Jacob cried out loudly, "No, no, not my Joseph!" Jacob cried and mourned for many days, and no one could comfort him.

Of course, Joseph was not dead. Sad and alone, missing his dad and his brothers, Joseph was living in Egypt as a slave to a very important man named Potiphar, who was a politician.

Potiphar saw something very special in Joseph and remarked, "You are wise and gifted." Joseph replied, "It is not me, but my God." Potiphar was intrigued by his answer and wanted to know more about Joseph's God. From that day forward, Potiphar grew to trust Joseph, and placed him in charge of all his servants and everything he owned.

Because of this, God made Potiphar even richer and more important in Egypt. Over the years Joseph still missed his family, but he continued to serve his God, worked very hard, and had a good life.

It so happened that Potiphar's wife, a very beautiful but wicked woman, told a terrible lie about Joseph to her husband that caused Joseph to be sent to prison. At first Joseph despaired.

Depressed, he cried to his God every day. God heard his calls and made him the favorite of all the prisoners, and soon Joseph was place head of all the other prisoners.

Pharaoh's baker and his butler were both imprisoned at that time, and one day Joseph remarked concerning their gloomy faces.

"Why so sad?" Joseph asked.

"We are having dreams, but cannot understand them," the men answered.

"My God allows me to understand dreams," Joseph said. "Tell me."

So they told Joseph their dreams, and he interpreted their meanings. To the butler he said, "In three days you will be working for the pharaoh again; please don't forget about me." But to the baker, he whispered, "In three days you will die."

In three days, both dreams came true. The butler was release, but did not remember Joseph once he left the prison. Jacob stayed in prison for two more years. Then one day the pharaoh had a troubling dream that no one could interpret, and the butler then remembered Joseph and told the story of his dream interpretations to the pharaoh. "His God helps him interpret dreams." The pharaoh released Joseph from prison and asked about his troubling dream.

"In the first, I saw seven heads of grain. They all grew from the same stem, and they were all healthy and full. But then I saw seven new heads of grain grow up from the same stalk. These were all thin and scorched. And then the seven thin heads of grain swallowed up the seven healthy ones."

"Egypt will have seven years of riches, then seven years of a dreadful famine," said Joseph. He advised the pharaoh to store enough food during the rich years for the famine years to come. The pharaoh was very impressed. "Your God is with you," he exclaimed. "I will place you in charge of Egypt, second only to me."

After seven rich years, there were indeed seven years of famine. Thanks to Joseph's advice, Egypt was the only place in the world where food was not scarce.

Back home in Canaan, Joseph's father and brothers were not doing as well, as the famine had left them without food. Jacob had heard that Egypt had food to sell, so he asked his older sons to go to Egypt to see what they could buy. Upon arriving in Egypt, the brothers approached the person in charge and bowed as a sign of respect, not recognizing the man as Joseph, their younger brother. Joseph recognized them, however, and at that very moment he remembered his boyhood dream that his brothers would bow to him. Still, he did not reveal his identity. In exchange for food, Joseph demanded that one of the brothers stay behind when the others left.

Joseph said harshly, "I will keep Simeon here. I need you to bring your youngest brother so I will know that you are not spies sent here to harm Egypt."

On the way back home, Judah cried out, "We are being punished for selling Joseph."

"We cannot take our youngest brother Benjamin to that cruel lord. Dad will die if he loses another son." But when the brothers told their father what had happened, Jacob agreed to let Benjamin go, after agonizing and praying for answered on what to do.

When Joseph saw Benjamin, he was elated. That night he held a great feast. Still keeping his identity secret, he ordered the brothers to return home to their father, but to leave Benjamin behind. Judah cried out, "No, please don't make us do that! You see, our dad lost his son Joseph, and could not bear to lose his youngest son, Benjamin. Please take me instead."

At that moment Joseph knew that his brothers were sorry for what they had done to him years before and he began to cry. He ordered his Egyptian servants to leave the room, then revealed to his brothers his true identity. His brothers were afraid that Joseph would harm them for revenge, but instead he embraced them. "The God of our fathers sent me here to save our family; it was God's plan, not yours," cried Joseph.

Joseph could not wait to see his dad. The next morning he called out instructions. "Get chariots and men, go to the land of Canaan, and bring my father back here to me." And so it was then Jacob was united with his favorite son Joseph and the entire family moved to Egypt and became very prosperous, all because there had indeed been something special about Joseph. When Joseph died, all of Egypt mourned for him, both Egyptians and Israelites alike. The God of the Israelites had used Joseph to save his people from a terrible famine.

"Children Love Eyeseeme Products"

Children need to have a sense of their own history in order to understand who they are. When children see the many contributions and accomplishments of people who look like them, they begin to believe in their own limitless potential.

<u>Other Books</u>
- Abraham
- Creation
- Jacob
- Moses

<u>Other Products</u>
- Games
- Posters
- Jigsaw Puzzles

www.eyeseeme.com
customerservice@eyeseeme.com